COMMUNICATIONS

Ian Graham

HODDER
Wayland

SCIENCE FACT FILES

COMMUNICATIONS · CRIMINAL INVESTIGATION
THE EARTH'S RESOURCES · ELECTRICITY AND MAGNETISM
FORCES AND MOTION · GENETICS
THE HUMAN BODY · LIGHT AND SOUND
THE SOLAR SYSTEM · WEATHER

Produced by Roger Coote Publishing
Gissing's Farm, Fressingfield
Suffolk IP21 5SH

Design and Typesetting Sarah Crouch
Commissioning Editor Lisa Edwards
Editor Sarah Doughty
Picture Researcher Lynda Lines
Illustrator Alex Pang
Text Consultant Dr. Mike Goldsmith

© 2001 Hodder Wayland

Published in Great Britain in 2001 by Hodder Wayland, an imprint of
Hodder Children's Books.

Endpaper picture: Optical fibres
Title page picture: Radio telescope dishes

We are grateful to the following for permission to reproduce photographs:
Corbis *cover* bottom & 16 (Joel W. Rogers); Digital Vision *cover* main, *endpapers*, 14 right;
Kodak 40 (all); Mary Evans Picture Library 34 right; Gettyone Stone *title page*, 8 top (Terry
Vine), 9 (Robert E. Daemmrich), 20 (Matthew McVay), 22 (Chad Slattery), 23 (Ross Harrison
Koty), 28/29 bottom (Peter Pearson), 37 (Andrew Errington), 39 (Bob Schatz); Olympus 41;
Science Photo Library *cover* top (Laguna Design), 8 bottom (David Ducros), 10 both (Jean-
Loup Charmet), 12 (Library of Congress), 14 left, 19 top (Simon Fraser), bottom (Philippe
Phailly), 21 (NASA), 24 top (NASA), 24 bottom (David A. Hardy), 25 (NASA), 26 (David
Parker), 27 left (ESA EURIMAGE), 27 right (ESA), 28 top (NRAO/AUI), 29 top, 30 (Julian
Baum), 31 left (Dr. Seth Shostak), 31 right (David Parker), 33 (Peter Menzel), 34 (Will & Deni
McIntyre), 38 (David Parker); Sony 32; Williams F1 15 (all).

ISBN 0 7500 3011 9

A catalogue record for this book is available from the British Library.

Printed in Hong Kong by Wing King Tong

Hodder Children's Books
A division of Hodder Headline Ltd
338 Euston Road, London NW1 3BH

CONTENTS

The words that are explained in the glossary are printed
in **bold** the first time they are mentioned in the text.

INTRODUCTION

Workers in modern offices rely on telecommunications to keep in touch with their own and other businesses.

Communication means exchanging ideas and information. Humans developed language and then writing to express themselves. The invention of printing allowed ideas and information to be copied on to paper many times so that large numbers of people could read them. Today, new technology means that we can now communicate with each other in more ways than at any time in the whole of human history. We can pick up a telephone and speak to someone in another country. We can watch a football match being played far away live on television – the sound and pictures can be relayed around the world by **satellites** in space. We can use mobile phones to keep in touch while on the move. E-mail and the **World Wide Web** allow us to communicate through our computers. Documents can be sent by telephone, using a fax machine. We can even see and hear astronauts on board their spacecraft as they orbit the Earth.

Telecommunications

Communication over long distances using electricity, light or radio waves is called telecommunication.

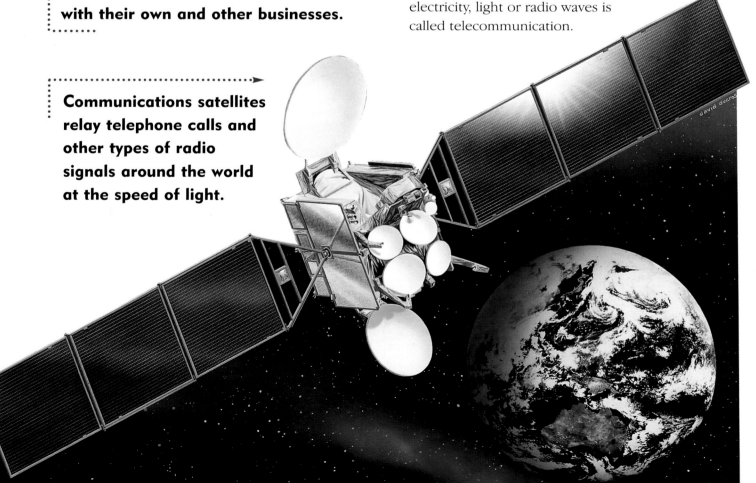

Communications satellites relay telephone calls and other types of radio signals around the world at the speed of light.

> **Telecommunications systems bring television pictures and sound into our homes.**

Most of today's long-distance communication is electronic. Telecommunications are very fast because they travel as **electric currents** or **electromagnetic** waves (radio or light). Telecommunications may be sent in the form of a gradually changing electromagnetic signal. This is called an analogue system, but increasingly nowadays, most telecommunications signals are digital. A digital signal is a stream of electrical or electromagnetic pulses that contain all the information in a coded form. This code represents speech, pictures, text or sound.

Telecommunication technology has changed our world. When Christopher Columbus (1451–1506) made his voyages of discovery to the New World, it took more than a month to carry a message across the Atlantic Ocean by ship. Today, the same message can be carried across the ocean in a fraction of a second.

HISTORY FILE

THE FIRST TELEGRAPH

In 1793, Frenchman Claude Chappe demonstrated a way of sending messages over long distances between towers on hilltops. He also invented the word 'telegraph' to describe it, from two Greek words meaning 'to write at a distance'. The Chappe telegraph sent coded messages across the countryside. Metal arms on the tops of the towers relayed the message from one hilltop to the next, using semaphore.

Chappe's invention created a lot of interest across Europe, although sadly for Chappe, it was never used commercially. However, today semaphore flags developed from Chappe's methods are still kept aboard naval ships.

TELEGRAPHY

HISTORY FILE

MORSE CODE

In the USA in the 1830s, Samuel Morse (1791–1872) produced a way of transmitting messages by cable – by inventing a code of dots and dashes, short and long bleeps, that enabled complicated messages to be sent more quickly. He set up a telegraph machine, and in 1844, in the USA, Morse used his telegraph system and code to send the first telegraph message. It ran for 64 km from Washington, D.C. to Baltimore, and said 'What hath God wrought!'

The Morse tapper (inset) and receiver.

Morse code

A	• —	T	—
B	— • • •	U	• • —
C	— • — •	V	• • • —
D	— • •	W	• — —
E	•	X	— • • —
F	• • — •	Y	— • — —
G	— — •	Z	— — • •
H	• • • •		
I	• •	1	• — — — —
J	• — — —	2	• • — — —
K	— • —	3	• • • — —
L	• — • •	4	• • • • —
M	— —	5	• • • • •
N	— •	6	— • • • •
O	— — —	7	— — • • •
P	• — — •	8	— — — • •
Q	— — • —	9	— — — — •
R	• — •	10	— — — — —
S	• • •		

Alessandro Volta demonstrates how his electric cell, or voltaic pile, could provide a steady supply of electricity.

For most of history and before the invention of the telegraph, we were only able to communicate by sight and sound – that is, by visual and acoustic methods using signals such as beacon fires or bells. By the end of the eighteenth century, scientists had discovered how to send electricity along wires to join two separate stations. The success of telegraphy depended on having a reliable source of electric current. Alessandro Volta (1745–1827), an Italian scientist, invented the vital component, the electric cell or battery needed for the telegraph. It was called a voltaic pile. Once the electricity could run along the wire it could be made to 'do' something at the other end of the wire, such as turning magnetic needles to point at letters.

By this means scientists had overcome the problem of how to detect pulses of electric current travelling along a wire. Using this simple system, messages could be sent along a single line as pulses of electric current. Each letter of the alphabet was represented by a different code of pulses. These pulses could travel over long distances very quickly.

From the 1830s, railways used the new electric telegraph to send information about trains to stations further down the railway line. The public were invited to come and see this new technical marvel. For a small price, they could even send their own telegraphic messages, called telegrams.

The Spreading Network

Thousands of kilometres of telegraph wire were strung between poles, linking towns and cities. The telegraph **networks** of mainland Europe and Britain were connected together by undersea cable in 1851. By 1854, the world's telegraph networks contained 37,000 km of wire, of which 25,000 km were laid in the USA. In 1861, the transcontinental telegraph line linked the east and west coasts of the USA. In 1866, the telegraph networks of Britain and the USA were linked together by laying cables across the bottom of the Atlantic Ocean.

TEST FILE

MORSE PRACTICE KEY

You can make a telegraph key by connecting a battery to a torch bulb and switch. Make the switch from two strips of cardboard with aluminium foil wrapped around them. Fix both strips to a board so that they overlap. Bend one up to form the key. Connect one strip to the battery. Connect the other strip to the bulb.

Finally, connect the other side of the battery to the bulb. Now, when you press the key, it completes the circuit and switches the bulb on.

You can practise sending Morse code messages yourself by making a Morse practice key from a bulb, a battery and a home-made switch.

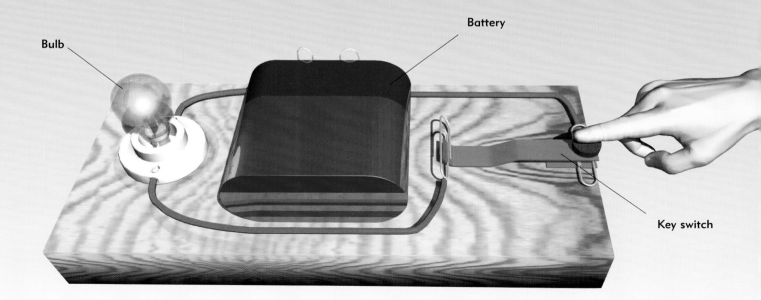

Bulb

Battery

Key switch

TELEPHONE

Soon after the electric telegraph was invented, experimenters started trying to send the human voice by a similar system. They had to find a way to change sound into an electric current and back to sound again. Scottish-born Alexander Graham Bell (1847–1922) solved the problem. His family was experienced in speech training and Bell's father had taught deaf people to speak. Bell moved to the USA to continue his father's work. His knowledge of sound and voice production, together with an interest in the newly invented telegraph, led him to experiment with sending sound by telegraph and invent the telephone.

Bell's Invention

Bell's telephone consisted of a thin metal sheet covering the end of a tube. A metal needle, attached to the sheet was dipped into a pot of acid. The size of an electric current passing through the needle and acid depended on how deeply the needle was dipped.

▲ **Alexander Graham Bell demonstrates his invention at the opening of the New York to Chicago telephone line in 1892.**

Speaking into the tube made the metal sheet vibrate. The needle fixed to it vibrated too, and made the electric current passing through the acid change in time with the voice.

At the other end of the telephone wire, the vibrating electric current flowed through a coil of wire wrapped around a piece of iron, forming a type of magnet called an electromagnet. The varying electric current changed the magnetic force of the electromagnet, which was next to a thin metal sheet. The changing magnetic force made the sheet vibrate and produce sound.

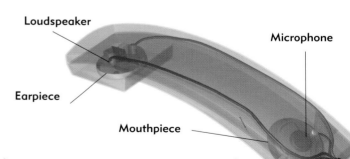

Loudspeaker

Microphone

Earpiece

Mouthpiece

▶ **A telephone handset contains a microphone in the mouthpiece, to change sound into electricity, and a loudspeaker in the earpiece, to change electricity into sound.**

FACT FILE

TELEPHONE NUMBERS
Every telephone in the world has its own unique number. The number has three parts – a country code, an area code and a local telephone number. When an international call is made, computers in the telephone exchange detect the country code and connect the call to the right country. Most countries are divided into smaller areas. If an area code is detected, the call is passed on to the right area. Finally, the call is connected to the telephone identified by the last part of the number.

1 –	202 –	111 1111
Country code	Area code	Number of person or organization
(1=USA)	(202= Washington, D.C.)	

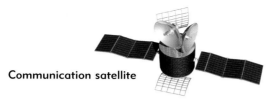

Communication satellite

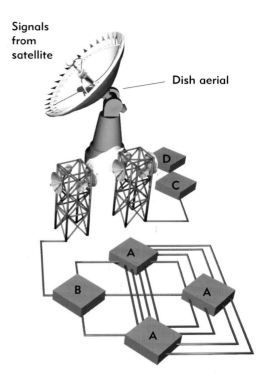

Signals to satellite

Dish aerial

International exchange (D)

Long-distance exchange (C)

Regional exchange (B)

Local exchange (A)

Subscribers

Signals from satellite

Dish aerial

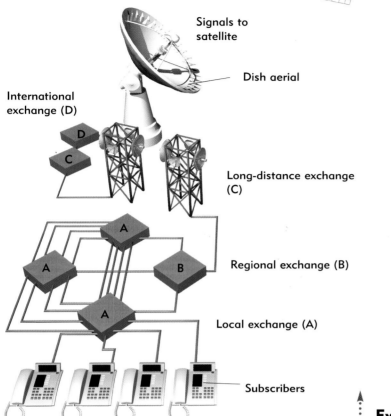

On 7 March 1876, Bell was granted a patent in the USA for his new machine – the telephone. Three days later, he made the world's first telephone call. His assistant, Thomas Watson, heard Bell's voice coming from the machine, saying 'Mr Watson, come here, I want to see you!'

Within two years, telephones were on sale to the public, although in the 1870s, only wealthy people could afford to buy them. Bell also brought his telephone to Britain and a public service was opened within two years.

Connecting the Calls

If two people are to talk to each other by telephone, the wire from one telephone has to be connected to the wire leading to the other telephone. At first, every call had to be connected by hand, by people called telephone operators. In 1891 Almon Brown Strowger, a funeral parlour owner from Kansas City, USA, invented a switch that connected telephone calls automatically. Strowger switches and other similar switches

Every telephone in every home and office is linked to every other telephone in the world through a network of exchanges and radio links.

remained in use until electronic switches began to replace them in the 1970s. Today, computerized switches connect our telephone calls.

Facsimile Transmission

Fax, or facsimile transmission, is a system for sending documents by telephone. As a sheet of paper is moved slowly through the machine by an electric motor, a bright light shines on it. The white paper reflects a lot of light, while dark printing or handwriting reflects less light. A light detector whizzes to and fro across the paper, detecting the reflections, line by line, and turning them into an electric current. The brighter the reflection, the bigger the current. Another machine receiving the call uses this electric current to control a printer, which prints a copy of the document.

RADIO

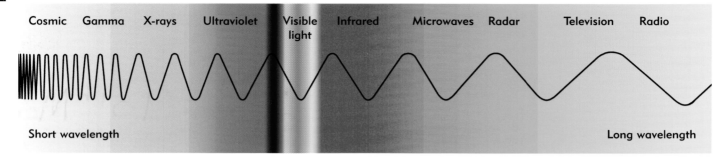

| Cosmic | Gamma | X-rays | Ultraviolet | Visible light | Infrared | Microwaves | Radar | Television | Radio |

Short wavelength

Long wavelength

Radio is used to carry information over long distances at the speed of light. Our world is criss-crossed with millions of invisible radio signals. They range from the voices of police officers, ambulance crews, firefighters, pilots and sailors to satellite signals, radio and television programmes and computer data.

The electromagnetic spectrum contains light and radio waves.

The First Uses of Radio

One of the first uses for radio was communication between ships and the shore. The messages were sent in Morse code by turning a radio signal on and off to make long and short bleeps. Voices could not be transmitted in this simple way. Instead, a voice was changed into an electric current that then changed, or **modulated**. The size of a radio signal is called a **carrier wave**. When the modulated wave was received, the carrier wave was taken away, leaving the voice signal, which was then changed into sound.

Soldiers keep in touch with their commanders by radio.

HISTORY FILE

WIRELESS TELEGRAPHY

Heinrich Hertz (1857–1894) was a German scientist and the first person to broadcast and receive radio waves. Within a year of reading about the discovery of radio waves, Guglielmo Marconi (1874–1937), an Italian scientist, succeeded in using them to communicate over a distance of nearly 2 km. Little interest was shown in his invention, so he developed it himself into 'wireless telegraphy'. By 1901, Marconi could send messages across the Atlantic Ocean – the beginning of worldwide radio communications.

Guglielmo Marconi, inventor of the radio.

Radio has many more uses than telegraphy and voice communication. The movements of animals in the wild are sometimes studied by fitting an animal with a collar that transmits a radio signal. Elephants, tigers and polar bears have been tracked in this way. Radio tracking devices are becoming so small now that in future they could be used to track everything from cars and personal computers to pets and even people. Pets might have radio trackers clipped to their collars so that they could be found if they were to escape. Children might have devices sewn into their clothes so that they could be located if they became separated from their parents on holiday or in crowds.

Telemetry

When the first modern peacetime rockets were launched in the 1950s and 1960s, scientists and engineers needed information about how well they were performing, so they could improve the design. This was done by fitting the rockets with sensors that sent measurements, such as height, speed and direction, to radio **receivers** on the ground. Taking measurements from a distance like this is called **telemetry**. Telemetry is still used today.

FACT FILE

WHAT IS A RADIO WAVE?
A radio wave is made from electricity and magnetism travelling through space together. Because of this, it is called an electromagnetic wave. The length of a wave is its **wavelength** and the number of waves that pass by in a second is its **frequency**. Light is another type of electromagnetic wave. The only difference between light and radio is the length of the waves. Radio waves are about a million times longer. All electromagnetic waves travel at the speed of light – 300,000 km per second. At that speed, you could fly around the world more than seven times in one second.

When the Thrust SuperSonic Car (SSC) set the first supersonic land speed record in 1997, the car bristled with sensors transmitting data about how well hundreds of its parts were working. Racing cars are also fitted with sensors that transmit information about the cars to their teams in the pits.

The racing cars' engineers watch their computer screens.

Racing drivers send information to their teams in the pits.

Racing drivers communicate with their teams by radio.

MOBILE TELEPHONES

Millions of people use mobile phones to keep in touch while they are on the move. Mobile phones are linked to the rest of the international telephone network by radio. Each handset contains a miniature radio **transmitter** and receiver.

The Cellular Phone

Mobile phones are also called cellular phones because the area they work in is divided into a series of smaller areas called cells. Each cell has its own radio aerial, or base station, with its own radio frequency. Cells next to each other use different frequencies. As soon as a mobile telephone is switched on, it sends a signal that is picked up by the nearest base station, letting the network know where it is. Every few minutes, the phone reports in like this, to keep the network up to date with its location. When a mobile phone moves from one cell to another during a call, the base station that was handling the call sends a radio signal alerting the surrounding base stations. The one serving the area the phone has moved into signals the central exchange, which tells the phone to switch to the new base station's radio frequency.

With a mobile phone, calls can be made anywhere within the cellular network.

To make a call, the mobile phone transmits the number dialled to the nearest base station, which sends it on to the mobile telephone exchange. Here, the call is connected to the correct telephone. The callers' voices are carried to and from the mobile phone by radio.

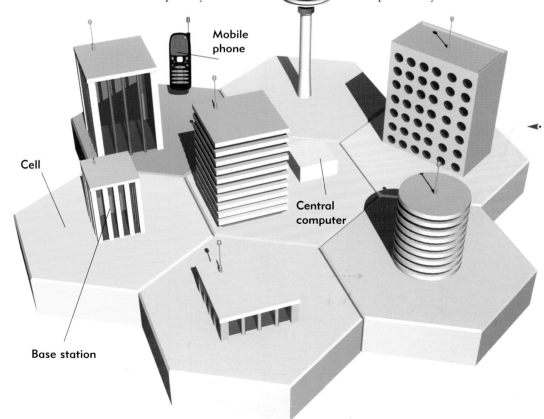

Mobile phone

Cell

Central computer

Base station

Mobile phones are linked to other telephones by radio, using aerials in small areas called cells. A central computer controls the telephone calls within a small group of cells.

Other Information

The radio signals that carry a mobile phone caller's voice could carry other types of information. In theory, the signals could represent anything – not just sound, but also photographs, documents and so on. All that is required is the right equipment and programming. Many mobile phones are already programmed to send text messages, receive Web pages and can even do two-way video-conferencing and live video over the network.

With the phone set to text, or mail, mode, the number keys produce letters instead of numbers. As there are only ten number keys, and not all of them are used to generate letters, each key has to produce more than one letter. Pressing a key repeatedly brings up each letter in turn until the correct letter appears. The message builds up on the phone's screen, letter by letter. When the message is complete, it is sent.

FUTURE FILE

SATELLITE TELEPHONES
Today's mobile telephone systems depend on building hundreds of towers for radio aerials all over the countryside and in towns. Some of the future mobile phone systems that are being planned now rely on radio aerials in space instead of on the ground. A swarm of satellites orbiting near the Earth will relay mobile phone calls. The advantage of using satellites is that a mobile phone should work just as well everywhere on Earth.

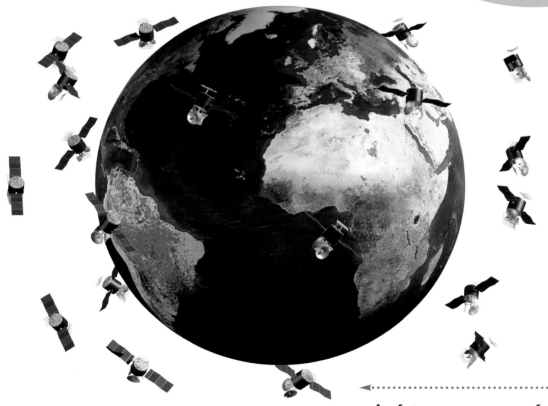

In future, a swarm of communications satellites orbiting the Earth may relay mobile telephone calls instead of thousands of aerials on the ground.

BROADCASTING

roadcasting is the transmission of radio and television programmes over a wide area so that anyone can receive them. Radio and television programmes are both transmitted by radio. The higher the frequency of a radio signal, the more information it can carry. Television programmes are transmitted at higher frequencies than radio programmes because their pictures contain much more information.

Radio

Radio programmes are sent in the same way as voice communications, by mixing the sound signal with a radio carrier wave. The sound signal changes the **amplitude** (size) of the carrier wave. This is called amplitude modulation (AM). In another method, called frequency modulation (FM), the frequency of the carrier wave is changed, or modulated. The FM system reduces the effects of interference from disturbances in the atmosphere.

> The colours in a television picture are caused by chemicals called phosphors. They glow when hit by electrons. A grille ensures that each beam of electrons hits only one colour of phosphor.

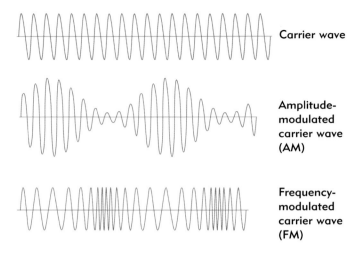

Carrier wave

Amplitude-modulated carrier wave (AM)

Frequency-modulated carrier wave (FM)

Sound signals and carrier waves are transmitted from a transmitting antenna at the speed of light (300,000 km/sec) and are picked up by receiving antennae.

Television

Transmitting television pictures is more complicated. The moving picture is made up from dozens of still pictures, which appear on the screen so quickly, one after another, that they seem to merge together to form one moving picture. Each still picture is made up of hundreds of lines traced out across the screen by beams of particles called electrons. The back of the TV screen is covered with thin strips of chemicals

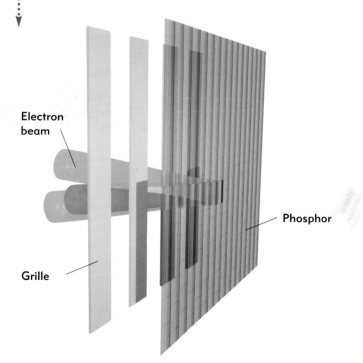

Electron beam

Grille

Phosphor

called phosphors. There are three types – one glows red when hit by electrons, one glows green and one glows blue. The strengths of the beams are varied by the television signal. As they scan back and forth across the screen, they make the red, green and blue strips glow. The coloured strips are so close together that they combine to make all the colours in the picture.

Cable and Satellite Television

There are three ways of receiving radio and television programmes nowadays – from transmitters on the ground, from transmitters on satellites in space and by underground cable. One satellite can transmit programmes to a whole country. To receive cable television, every house has to be connected to a cable buried under the street.

A dish-shaped aerial receives television programmes beamed down by satellites.

FUTURE FILE

HDTV
One way to make better quality television pictures is to squeeze more lines into the picture so that it can show the smallest details more clearly. This is called high definition television, or HDTV. Today, HDTV means a digital television system with pictures made of more than about 1,000 lines. Several HDTV systems have been demonstrated, but Japan is the only place where regular HDTV broadcasts have been made, using 1,125-line pictures.

Older cable systems used metal cables, but modern cable systems send out programmes as light beams travelling along glass cables.

TV Systems

The three main television systems in use today are PAL, SECAM and NTSC. PAL and SECAM, used in Europe, Russia, South America and Australia, produce 25 pictures per second and each picture is made of 625 lines. NTSC, used in the USA, Canada and Japan, produces 30 pictures per second, and each picture is made from 525 lines.

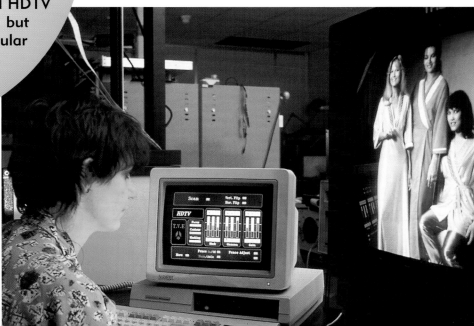

A technician uses a computer to adjust the quality of a HDTV image. The format and resolution of the image resemble that of a cinema picture.

RADAR

Air traffic controllers follow aircraft movements by air.

Radio waves probe the world around us and provide information about things we cannot see. Objects like planes and ships reflect radio waves and this is used to locate them and follow their movements from a distance. The system is called **radar**, which stands for RAdio Detection And Ranging.

How Radar Works
Radar works by sending out radio waves and picking up any reflections, or echoes, that bounce back from objects. The time taken for an echo to come back shows how far away the object is – the further away it is, the longer it takes for the echo to arrive. You can see the same effect if you bounce a ball against a wall.

HISTORY FILE

THE BIRTH OF RADAR
The possibility of locating objects by radio was discovered at the US Naval Research Laboratory in 1922, when a ship on the Potomac River in the USA caused a ripple in radio waves travelling from one aerial to another. In 1930, the effect was noticed again at the same laboratory when an aircraft flew through a radio beam. The world's first practical radar system was finally built in Britain in 1938 by a team under the leadership of Robert Watson-Watt.

The further away from the wall you are, the longer it takes the ball to bounce back. Radar works in the same way, using radio waves instead of a ball. But as radio waves travel at the speed of light, radar works very quickly indeed.

Radar is not only used to locate planes and ships. Ground-penetrating radar probes the ground and forms a map of what lies beneath the surface. Archaeologists use it to search for deeply buried objects. In the security industry, radar sets are used to detect movement in a room and sound an alarm if the room is broken into. Satellites use radar to probe a planet's surface.

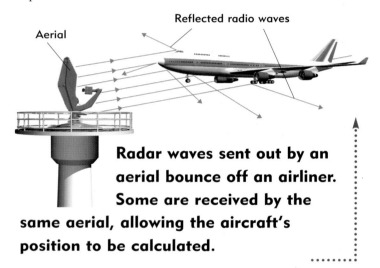

Radar waves sent out by an aerial bounce off an airliner. Some are received by the same aerial, allowing the aircraft's position to be calculated.

Measuring Speed
If radio waves of a certain length are fired at an object moving towards the transmitter, the reflected waves are shortened. If the object is moving away, the reflected waves are lengthened. And the faster the object is moving, the greater is the change in wavelength. This happens with sound waves too: you can hear it when an ambulance passes by sounding its siren. Coming towards you, the siren sounds higher and higher as the sound waves are shortened. Then it falls in pitch as the ambulance races away and the sound waves are lengthened. It is called the Doppler effect, and it is used to measure speed. Doppler radar is used by the police to make sure vehicles are not going faster than the speed limit. In industry, Doppler radar is used to measure the speed of objects moving along a conveyor belt or down a production line.

FACT FILE

MAPPING VENUS

The surface of the planet Venus is permanently hidden beneath thick clouds. The *Magellan* spacecraft orbited the planet between 1989 and 1994. It used radar to probe through the clouds and make a map of the surface. It fired several thousand radar pulses per second at the planet's surface and measured how long it took them to bounce back. A computer then changed the time interval into a height, gradually building up a map of the surface.

The *Magellan* spacecraft was deployed by the space shuttle *Atlantis* on 4 May 1989.

USA

Aircraft movements are tracked and guided by radar. Air traffic control uses radar in two different ways. Primary radar shows an aircraft's position, while secondary radar communicates with the aircraft and asks it for more information.

Primary and Secondary Radar

Primary radar works by sending radio waves out in all directions and detecting any reflections that bounce back. The reflections appear as glowing spots on a radar screen. Each spot corresponds to an aircraft and the position of the spot on the screen shows where the aircraft is – how far away and in which direction.

Secondary radar sends out a radio signal that is received by a device called a transponder inside the plane. A transponder is a transmitter-responder, a radio transmitter that sends out information automatically when it receives the correct radio signal. An airliner's transponder sends out the plane's call-sign, or code-name, and its height. This information appears on the radar screen next to the spot produced by primary radar.

The air traffic control tower at Los Angeles airport, USA.

Weather Radar

Airliners use radar in another way. An airliner's nose contains a radar dish that probes the sky up to 500 km ahead of the plane. The radar signals it sends out are reflected by moisture in the air like a car's headlight lighting up rain falling in front of it. The most moisture is found inside storm clouds, which appear on a screen in the cockpit. Pilots use this to give early warning of storms so that they can fly around them.

Military Radar

Military aircraft use radar to detect enemy planes. Some of the missiles they fire use radar to home in on enemy aircraft. Electronic Counter Measures (ECM) aircraft try to block the enemy's radar. They can even create false radar signals that appear on an enemy's radar screens as aircraft that are not really there at all.

FACT FILE

STEALTH PLANES

The spot that shows a plane's position on a radar screen is called the plane's radar signature. Designers of military planes have found ways of making an aircraft harder to detect by making its radar signature smaller. The plane's shape is carefully chosen to reflect radar waves away from the ground and it is coated with special material and paint that cut radar reflections even more. These measures are called stealth technology and planes that use them, like the *Lockheed F-117 Night Hawk*, are called stealth planes. There are now stealth ships too.

Lockheed F-117 Night Hawk planes in flight.

FUTURE FILE

IN-CAR RADAR

Future cars may use radar to prevent collisions. A radar set built into a car would be able to measure the distance to the vehicle in front very precisely. And if that distance began to fall very quickly, it may be because the cars are about to collide. The system could either alert the driver or automatically apply the car's brakes.

Cars fitted with radar could help drivers avoid collisions while driving or parking in tight spaces. The radar system could even take control of the car if it sensed that a collision was about to occur.

Radar waves

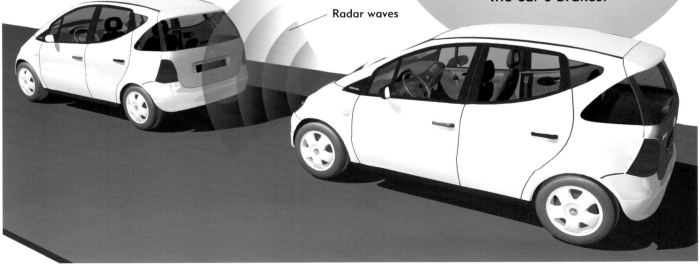

Shuttle astronauts talk to mission control by using communications satellites.

HISTORY FILE

THE FIRST SPACE RADIO

On 4 October 1957, the Soviet Union launched a small metal 'ball' into orbit around the Earth. It was the first-ever artificial satellite, *Sputnik 1*. It contained a radio transmitter that bleeped as it circled the world until its battery ran out of energy 21 days later. *Sputnik 1* re-entered the Earth's atmosphere and burned up after three months and 1,400 orbits.

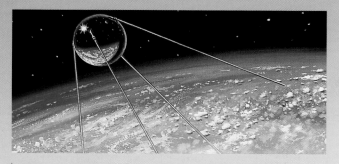

An artist's impression of *Sputnik 1*, orbiting the Earth.

Sound travels through the air as pressure waves. Hold your hand in front of a loudspeaker or over a drum and you may feel the pressure waves. Unlike light and other electromagnetic waves, sound waves cannot exist in a vacuum – they have to travel through something, because they are made from vibrations of particles of matter. Outside the Earth's atmosphere, there is very little matter, so sound waves cannot travel there. Space is silent. Radio waves are used to communicate with satellites and spacecraft because radio waves are waves of energy that can travel through empty space.

Space Delay

Radio communications on Earth seem instant, because radio waves travel so incredibly fast. At 300,000 km per second a radio wave can cross the USA from New York to Los Angeles, a distance of about 4,000 km, in just over one-hundredth of a second.

But even light-speed communications take a long time if the distances are big enough. A communications satellite orbits 36,000 km from the Earth. A telephone call connected by one of these satellites has to travel out to the satellite and back to Earth. A reply comes back via the same route – a total round trip of 144,000 km, which takes a radio signal about half a second. Sometimes, telephone calls are connected by two satellites, causing double the delay. These delays between saying something and hearing a reply can make long-distance telephone conversations difficult.

Deep Space Communications

The situation is more difficult when it comes to communicating with space probes in far-flung parts of the solar system. In 1997, the *Sojourner* rover vehicle explored part of the surface of Mars. Its movements were controlled from Earth, but it was impossible to 'drive' the rover by remote control at the same time as it was actually travelling across the Martian surface. This was because of the communications delay between Earth and Mars which meant that radio signals took 15 minutes to reach the rover. Imagine trying to ride a bicycle that only responded after 15 minutes! A detailed plan for the rover's movements was worked out each day and sent to its computer.

Radio signals took 15 minutes to reach the *Sojourner* rover on the surface of Mars.

The delays are even longer when space probes visit the outer planets. In 1981, as *Voyager 2* glided past the planet Saturn which is 1,200 million km from Earth, the radio signals that carried the photographs it took of the beautiful ringed planet travelled through the solar system for one hour and 26 minutes before they reached Earth.

FACT FILE

WAVES AROUND THE WORLD

The way that radio waves travel depends on how long they are. Very long radio waves, from 100 m to several hundred km long, hug the surface of the Earth, following its curved shape. Shorter waves travel in straight lines, but any that travel out into space are reflected back by a layer of electrically charged particles called the **ionosphere**. The shortest radio waves, between 8 mm and 20 m long, travel through the ionosphere and so these can be used to communicate with satellites and spacecraft.

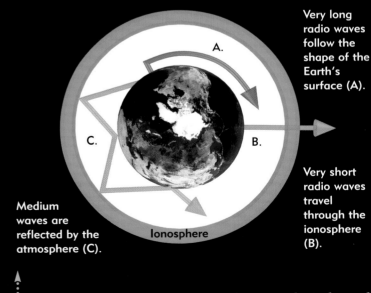

Very long radio waves follow the shape of the Earth's surface (A).

Very short radio waves travel through the ionosphere (B).

Medium waves are reflected by the atmosphere (C).

Ionosphere

Radio waves behave according to their length

A Global Positioning System (GPS) receiver pinpoints its position by using the radio signals it receives from satellites.

Comsats

Communications satellites, or comsats, have revolutionized telecommunications. Radio transmitters are often fitted to tall towers so that their signals are not blocked by hills or buildings. The higher the transmitter is, the further its signals can travel. A comsat is like a radio transmitter on top of a very tall tower, thousands of kilometres high. One satellite can transmit radio signals to a whole continent, replacing hundreds of transmitters on the ground.

A radio signal to be relayed by a comsat is first transmitted from the ground up to the satellite. This is called the **uplink**. An aerial on the satellite receives the signal, which is amplified before being transmitted back down to Earth. This is the **downlink**.

Watching the Earth

Until the 'space age', weather forecasters had to rely on scattered weather observations taken from ground stations, balloons, planes and ships. Now, thanks to satellite photographs, transmitted by radio signals, they can see whole weather systems forming and moving. Earth observation satellites measure the ocean currents and winds, study how we use land, monitor sea ice, and show up pollution in rivers and the sea.

M any of the everyday things we do depend on communicating with spacecraft. A growing number of people watch television programmes that are beamed into their homes from a satellite. News reports from all over the world for radio and television programmes are also relayed to broadcasters by satellites. Some long-distance telephone calls are connected by satellites. Navigation satellites of the Global Positioning System (GPS) enable pilots, sailors, explorers and others to plot their positions very accurately. Science satellites carry a variety of instruments and experiments. Weather forecasts depend on satellite photographs.

FACT FILE

STATIONARY ORBIT
Most communications satellites and some other types of satellites are placed in a special orbit called geostationary, or geosynchronous, orbit. A satellite orbiting at 36,000 km above the Equator travels round the Earth at the same speed as the Earth turns, so it stays over the same spot on the ground. Aerials on Earth that send radio signals to the satellite or receive signals from it can keep pointing in the same direction all the time.

Satellites watch the Earth 24 hours a day and take photographs that show the effects of weather, pollution, war, engineering, forestry and farming.

The European Remote-Sensing Satellite (ERS-1) uses radar to study the world's oceans.

Spy satellites watch military activities, to make sure that troops, ships or aircraft are not being moved in threatening or sinister ways.

Science in Space

A fleet of science satellites and space probes has been launched to study the planets and stars. They have landed on or flown past most of the planets. Planet scientists now have detailed maps and close-up photographs of most of the planets. Astronomers have gained an enormous amount of information from instruments in space. The *Hubble Space Telescope* has been able to take breathtaking photographs of stars, because it is outside the atmosphere. It is the Earth's atmosphere that makes the stars seems to twinkle and wobble. Other space telescopes study electromagnetic energy from the stars such as ultraviolet and X-rays, which are mostly blocked by the atmosphere.

HISTORY FILE

ARTHUR C. CLARKE
Arthur C. Clarke (1917–) was the first person to suggest using satellites to relay communications signals around the world. In 1945, he wrote an article entitled 'Extra-Terrestrial Relays' for the magazine *Wireless World*, which described the system. At the time, few people thought it would ever happen, but within 25 years the first communications satellites were orbiting the Earth just as Clarke had predicted.

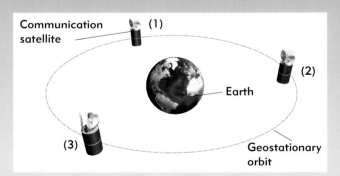

Communication satellite (1)

Earth

(2)

(3)

Geostationary orbit

Three communications satellites can relay radio signals between any two points anywhere on Earth.

SIGNALS FROM SPACE

We receive information from the rest of the Universe all the time – not messages from 'little green men', but energy from the stars. Astronomers learn about the Universe by studying this energy, its **wavelength**, its intensity and the ways in which it changes over time.

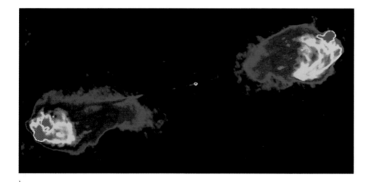

Natural radio signals are sent out by jets of matter blasted out of a distant galaxy.

Stars give out much more energy than just light. Natural radio signals given out by some stars, called pulsars, show how fast they are spinning. Radio signals from vast galaxies containing hundreds of billions of stars give clues about what is happening at their centre. Radio waves given out by clouds of gas in space show how fast the gas is moving and in which direction.

Radio Astronomy

Receiving and studying radio signals from space is called radio astronomy. The signals are received by large dish-shaped **antennae** called radio telescopes. Most radio telescopes are metal dishes that can be swivelled to point at any part of the sky. The world's biggest radio telescope is a 305 m dish built in a natural hollow in the ground in Arecibo, Puerto Rico.

Radio waves shorter than a centimetre or so are absorbed by water vapour in the Earth's atmosphere, while radio waves longer than about 20 m are reflected back into space by the ionosphere.

TEST FILE

SPACE RADIO
You can hear radio waves from space for yourself. Tune a radio or television set away from the broadcasting stations. Between the stations, you should hear a hissing or rushing noise. This noise is made by radio waves arriving from space.

HISTORY FILE

THE HISS MYSTERY

In 1928, a young engineer called Karl Jansky (1905–50), working at the Bell Telephone Laboratories in New Jersey, USA, was asked to investigate noises that were causing problems in ship-to-shore radio communications. He built a radio aerial to study all the unwanted noises. Most were caused by thunderstorms, but he discovered that the hissing noise he heard was caused by radio waves coming from space. Astronomers later discovered that they were coming from the direction of the centre of our galaxy, the Milky Way.

Karl Jansky started the science of radio astronomy.

Radio waves between one centimetre and 20 m long reach the ground, so these are the wavelengths that radio astronomers study.

Radio waves arriving from space are reflected off the radio telescope dish like light hitting a curved mirror, so that they come together at an aerial held over the centre of the dish. The tiny electric currents created in the aerial by the radio signals are amplified about 1,000 million million times. The telescope sweeps back and forth across part of the sky, measuring the strength of radio waves at each point, building up a picture, point by point.

The Very Large Array (VLA) of radio telescopes in New Mexico scan the sky.

EXPLORING THE STARS

When the first space probes were sent to tour the solar system, scientists knew that some of them would eventually leave the solar system and head out towards the stars. So, they were given messages that could be read by any intelligent creatures that find them, probably millions of years from now. Their discovery may be so far in the future that the civilization that finds them may not exist yet.

Radio messages have been sent out towards the stars too, but many of them are so far away that even if an answer comes back we may no longer be here to receive it.

The distance to the stars is measured in **light years**. A light year is the distance light travels in one year – over 9 million million km (travelling at a speed of 300,000 km/sec). The closest star (apart from the Sun) is about four light years away. A radio message sent today would take four years to reach it and an answer would take another four years to return. But the closest civilization capable of receiving and understanding our messages could be hundreds or even thousands of light years away.

An artist's impression of the space probe *Voyager 2* seen crossing the day–night boundary on Triton, Neptune's seventh moon.

SETI scientists search for a radio signal from an alien civilization.

Searching for Aliens

A more practical way of contacting an alien civilization is to listen for its radio signals. SETI (Search for Extra-Terrestrial Intelligence) work involves listening to radio signals from space in the hope of finding signals that come from intelligent creatures. Millions of different radio frequencies are scanned in the hope of finding one that might have come from an intelligent civilization.

TEST FILE

HELP SEARCH FOR ALIENS

You can take part in the search for extraterrestrial intelligence yourself. If you have access to the Internet, log on to the 'SETI at home' Web site (www.setiathome.ssl.berkeley.edu) and download the SETI program. Now, when your computer is idle, its screensaver will be the SETI program. It takes data received by the Arecibo radio telescope and analyzes it, searching for any trace of a signal that might have been sent by an alien intelligence. You might be the first person to discover a message from an extraterrestrial.

HISTORY FILE

EARTH CALLING

In 1974, a radio message was transmitted from the Arecibo radio telescope towards a galaxy called the M13 globular cluster, a distance of up to 25,000 light years away. It will take 25,000 years to get there ... and if there is anyone there to receive it, another 25,000 years for an answer to come back!

The Arecibo radio telescope.

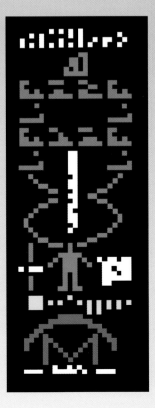

The Arecibo message was made up from 1,679 bits of information. When they are rearranged into a grid 23 bits across and 73 bits long, they make a pattern that contains information about the Earth, the human race and the genetic code that makes us what we are.

GOING DIGITAL

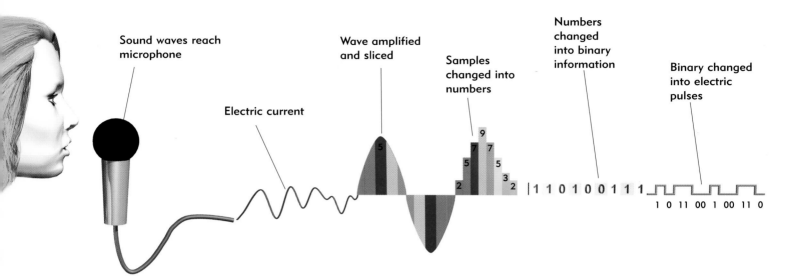

Sound waves reach microphone

Electric current

Wave amplified and sliced

Samples changed into numbers

Numbers changed into binary information

Binary changed into electric pulses

|1 1 0 1 0 0 1 1 1

1 0 11 00 1 00 11 0

Everything seems to be going digital – television, radio, telephones, recorded music. But what does 'going digital' actually mean? Before digital technology, a television signal was a copy, in radio waves, of the pictures being transmitted. If the waves were distorted, perhaps because of bad weather or interference from other radio signals, the receiver could not tell the difference between the perfect and the faulty waves. It changed them all into pictures, so the pictures were distorted too.

A digital television signal is different. It is made from radio waves, but the waves represent a code of numbers, called **binary code**. Binary code contains only two numbers – zero and one. The code tells the television set how to create the pictures.

A microphone changes sound into a wave-like electric current. The size of the wave is measured thousands of times a second. This is changed into a binary number, which finally becomes a stream of electric pulses.

Even if the radio waves carrying the code are distorted, it doesn't matter. As long as the television set can find the code in the distorted waves, it can produce perfect pictures, because it is the code, not the waves themselves, that contain the picture information.

Communicating with Digits

Digital technology not only improves television reception, it also makes telephone calls clearer and improves the quality of sound recordings. Digital discs and tapes contain a code, which the player uses to create sound. Crackles, hisses and other unwanted noises caused by the player, its electronics or minor damage and wear to the tape or disc, are not changed into sound.

Digital technology is increasingly popular because it uses the same sort of code that computers use, so digital information can be stored and processed very quickly by standard computer systems.

A Digital Versatile Disc (DVD) player plays laser discs which are also called DVDs. Laser discs are the same size as CDs, but a DVD can hold a whole movie.

It also means that all sorts of information – printed text, sounds and pictures – can be sent together through the same digital communications channel instead of having to use a variety of different communications methods such as post, fax, radio and telephone.

When an image is changed into the same digital code that a computer uses, it can be stored, processed and displayed by a computer.

TEST FILE

BINARY NUMBERS

All numbers can be changed into binary form. Each column of a decimal number is worth ten times the one to its right, so the columns are units, 10s, 100s and so on. The binary system uses only two digits: 0 and 1. With a binary number the units digit has the value one, the next digit to its left is two times larger, and the next is two times larger than that. So the columns are units, 2s, 4s, 8s, and so on.

The binary number 101, has a '1' in the '4s' column, a '0' in the '2s' column and a '1' in the units column. It makes a total of five in the decimal system.

Here are the first ten numbers from zero in decimal and also binary.

Decimal	Binary
0	0000
1	0001
2	0010
3	0011
4	0100
5	0101
6	0110
7	0111
8	1000
9	1001

Binary numbers can be added together just like decimal numbers. Try adding the binary numbers 0110 and 0011. Remember, in binary, 1 + 1 = 10, not 2.

0110 is the same as the decimal number 6 and 0011 is the same as 3, so the answer should be the same as 9 and that is 1001.

OPTICAL FIBRES

A network of glass telecommunications cables has spread around the world. They carry telephone calls, radio and television programmes and computer data over land and under the sea.

The first telegraph and telephone cables were made from metal, because they had to carry electric currents. In the 1960s, electrical engineers suggested using cables made from glass instead of metal, carrying information as beams of light instead of electric currents. The glass was in the form of hair-thin fibres of ultra-pure glass – so pure that a beam of light could travel through 100 km of the cable without fading.

HISTORY FILE

COMMUNICATING BY LIGHT

Light has been used for communication since long before the laser and optical fibres were invented. In the nineteenth century, a device called a heliograph used a mirror to reflect sunlight. Opening and closing a shutter interrupted the beam, making the light flash in Morse code. During the Second World War (1939–45), a device called an Aldis lamp was used to signal between ships. It was like a heliograph, but used light from a bulb instead of sunlight.

A double heliograph used by the navy to reflect sunlight.

Light shines from the ends of the fibres in an optical cable.

The Advantage of Light

The first optical telecommunications cables were used in the 1970s, and the first undersea optical cables in the 1980s. They have now replaced most long-distance metal communications cables. Their use spread quickly because they could carry so much more information in thinner, lighter cables. The first optical telephone cable could carry 2,000 calls. Now, one fibre can carry 20,000 telephone calls and a whole cable, such as an undersea optical communications cable, can carry more than one million telephone calls. As optical cables do not carry electric currents, they are not affected by electrical interference. Another advantage is that the material optical cables are made from is far less expensive than the copper of metal cables. Optical telecommunications cables are made from glass, which is made by melting sand.

Optical cables for shorter links, inside a building for example, are often made from plastic. Plastic optical fibres are less expensive to make than glass fibres and they are more flexible. They are not used for long-distance links, because light fades more quickly in plastic than glass.

INSIDE AN OPTICAL FIBRE
An optical fibre is not just a simple thread of glass. It has a glass core, through which the light travels, surrounded by a cladding, made from a different type of glass. The cladding stops the light from escaping from the core. Light travels through the core like water through a pipe. Optical fibres are sometimes called light pipes. Each fibre, or group of fibres, in an optical cable is protected by a plastic sleeve to stop it being damaged by rubbing against the other fibres. Steel wire runs down the centre of the cable to give it extra strength.

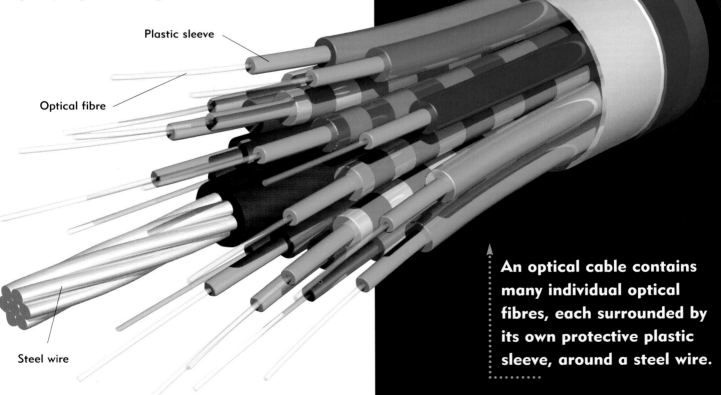

Plastic sleeve

Optical fibre

Steel wire

An optical cable contains many individual optical fibres, each surrounded by its own protective plastic sleeve, around a steel wire.

THE INTERNET

The Internet is a global computer network made from hundreds of smaller networks linked together by cables, telephone lines and satellites. Anyone can connect their computer to the Internet and look at information stored in computers all over the world.

The World Wide Web

The Internet itself is just a bunch of computers connected together. It is the World Wide Web that makes the Internet so easy to use. The Web contains millions of pages of information. A group of pages created by one organization is called a Web site. Pages from different Web sites are linked together electronically. There is no need to know where in the world the pages are stored. Clicking on a link, which might be a highlighted word, a picture or a button, takes you to the next page, which appears almost immediately. Web pages are created using a special computer language called hypertext mark-up language (html), so a program called a browser is needed to access and view them.

Every Web site has its own unique address that tells the Internet where to find it.

http://www.sitename@domain

The part that is 'http' tells the browser to connect to a Web page. The part that is 'www' indicates that it is the World Wide Web. Not all Web site names include this. The 'sitename' is the name of the web site. The 'domain' is the name of the organization whose computer holds the Web site. The last part of the domain name shows what sort of organization it is and, sometimes, where it is. The '.com.' part indicates a commercial organization. There may also be a two-letter code to show which country the web site comes from – '.uk' for the United Kingdom or '.au' for Australia, for example.

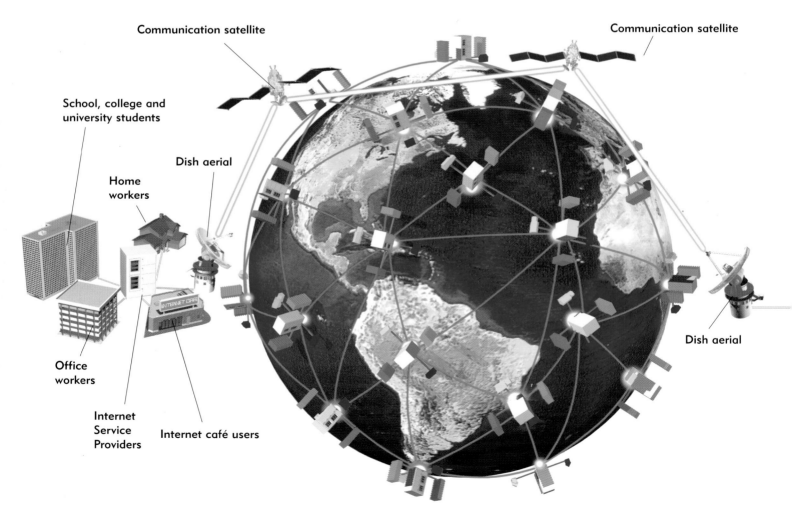

Communication satellite

Communication satellite

School, college and university students

Dish aerial

Home workers

Office workers

Internet Service Providers

Internet café users

Dish aerial

Going Online

Access to the Internet and Web is provided by companies called Internet Service Providers (ISPs). Computers are connected to the Internet through an Internet Service Provider by telephone or by cable. Businesses and other organizations are usually connected by cable, while most home users are connected by telephone. Some cable television companies offer Internet connections using the same cable that brings television programmes into the home.

Telephones are designed to carry voices and other sounds, but not digital computer data. So, when a computer is connected to the Internet by telephone, a device called a **modem**, or modulator-demodulator, is needed to change the computer data into a different form that can be sent by telephone. The modem changes the 0s and 1s of the computer's digital language into musical notes. It also receives musical notes from other computers and changes them back into digital code, which it passes on to the computer.

Some cafés are equipped with computer terminals that customers can use to surf the World Wide Web.

The Internet is a global network of computers linked by cables and satellites that anyone can connect their own computer to.

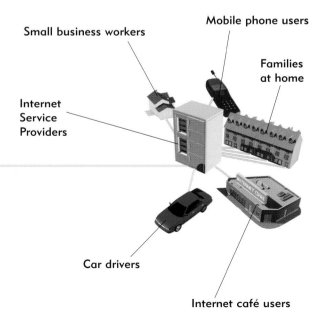

Small business workers
Mobile phone users
Families at home
Internet Service Providers
Car drivers
Internet café users

HISTORY FILE

HOW DID THE INTERNET BEGIN?
In the 1960s, scientists in the USA needed a way to connect the computers at their universities and laboratories together so that they could share information. They were worried that a system controlled by one computer could be destroyed too easily by an enemy during a war. So, they designed a network, called ARPAnet (after the Advanced Research Projects Agency), that could carry on working even if parts of it were damaged. In the 1980s, it was taken over by the US National Science Foundation, which improved it and allowed more people to connect their computers to it. During the 1990s, the Internet, as it was known by then, was finally opened up for anyone to use.

By the end of the 1990s the Internet and World Wide Web had become so popular and so widely used that many businesses depended on them for communication and also for advertising and selling their products and services. The World Wide Web contains information about practically every subject imaginable, so it can be used as a vast library. The latest news appears on the Web moments after events have happened. Anyone can keep right up to date with what is happening in the world without having to wait for the next news report on radio or television.

FACT FILE

WEB FACTS AND FIGURES
There are about 10 million Web sites on the World Wide Web and the number is growing all the time. They contain more than one billion pages. It is impossible for anyone to read them all in one lifetime. It would take about 500 years!

A computer scientist updates pages on the World Wide Web, at CERN, the European particle physics laboratory in Geneva, Switzerland. The Web was created at CERN and services started in 1989.

Searching the Web
There is so much information on the Web that finding the one or two Web sites you want amongst the millions of others seems to be an impossible task. Special programs called 'search engines' are essential for finding Web sites. When a word or phrase is keyed into the search engine, it hunts through a file of key information about each site within a few seconds and produces a list of the sites that are most likely to contain what you are looking for. It will also rank them depending on how many references to your search they contained. Clicking on a site on the list takes you straight to it. A variety of search engines are available on the Web. Each has its own Web site.

Web pages can include graphics, photographs, animation, video and sound. Each of them has to be digitized – that is, changed into digital code. When a computer downloads the code for a photograph or video clip from the Web, it must change the code back into a photograph or video clip in the correct way. So, Web browsers have programs built into them to do this. From time to time, new ways of creating sound, graphics, video and other types of information are developed. The new programs needed to decode them can be added to Web browsers by downloading them from the Internet. They are called plug-ins.

Pictures to a computer

Pictures from a computer

E-mail

Electronic messages, or e-mail, can be sent through the Internet to any of the millions of people who are connected to it. Everyone who connects to the Internet is given an electronic address so that e-mails are received only by the person they are addressed to.

Username@provider

The 'username' is the name of the person or organization the e-mail is sent to and 'provider' is the name of their Internet Service Provider.

E-mails can only contain simple text, but many people want to send more complicated documents prepared using word processing programs. These can be sent as 'e-mail attachments'. An attachment is a document that is linked to an e-mail and travels with it. When the e-mail is sent, it travels through the telephone network to the Internet Service

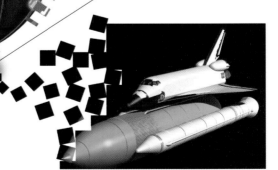

Provider named in the e-mail address. There, it is stored in an electronic mailbox or pigeon-hole – a file in the Internet Service Provider's computer. The next time the person the e-mail is addressed to connects to the Internet, he or she can collect the e-mail by downloading it into his or her computer.

DIGITAL IMAGING

When photography began, in the nineteenth century, images were made on light-sensitive glass or metal plates, which had to be treated with chemicals to make the pictures appear on them. Later, film replaced the plates. Today, film still has to be developed chemically. But now there is another type of photography that doesn't use any film at all – digital photography.

A digital camera looks like a photographic camera. It has a lens to focus light and a shutter that opens to let light into the camera. But instead of film, it has a light-sensitive chip called a CCD (Charge-Coupled Device). The CCD changes light into electricity. The surface of a CCD is divided into tiny squares called pixels. When light hits the CCD, an electric charge builds up on each pixel, like piling up coins on the squares of a chess board. The brighter the light, the bigger the charge.

The size of the electric charge on each pixel is changed into a number. The bigger the charge, the bigger the number. The numbers are then changed into binary code. The code for each pixel contains 24 bits (binary digits – 0s and 1s), eight for the amount of red light hitting the pixel, eight for the amount of green and eight for blue.

Flashgun

Shutter release button

Lens

A digital camera looks similar to a traditional camera, but it takes photographs without using film.

Control functions

Eyepiece

The memory card stores the images made by the digital camera.

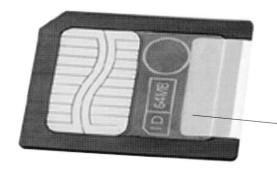

Memory card

LCD screen

Battery casing

40

Light-sensitive surface

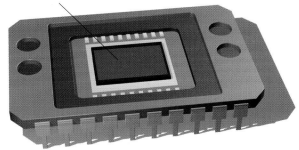

Instead of film, a digital camera has a light-sensitive chip called a Charge Coupled Device (CCD).

HISTORY FILE

THE FIRST PHOTOGRAPH
The French inventor Joseph-Nicéphore Niepce (1765–1833) made the first permanent photograph in 1826. It showed the view from his workroom. The metal photographic plate he used had to be exposed to light for eight hours to record the image.

Most digital cameras store the photographs they take on a memory card that plugs into the camera. The card contains a computer memory chip. A few digital cameras store photographs on a floppy disk. Once an image has been changed into digital code, it can be stored, changed and communicated in the same way as computer data.

Resolution
The more pixels a CCD has, the more detail its photographs contain. A digital camera designed for holiday snaps might have a 640 x 480 pixel CCD. Its images are made from 640 spots of colour across by 480 spots down. A professional digital camera taking high-quality photographs might have a 1,600 x 1,200 pixel CCD.

Slimming the Bits
An image contains an enormous amount of detail. Even a 640 x 480 CCD makes pictures containing more than seven million bits of information. To cut down the amount of information, so that more pictures can be stored on each memory card, some of the information is thrown away. It's called data compression. Data compression is also used in telecommunications to slim down the amount of information that has to be moved from place to place.

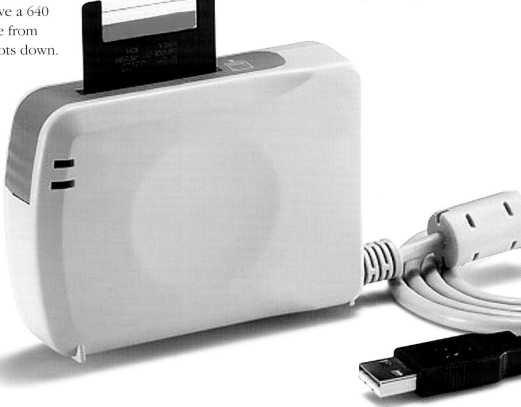

Digital cameras can supply images to a computer along a cable via an external card drive.

MOTION PICTURES

Motion pictures communicate more information than the printed word or a still picture. Film captures movement because of an effect called 'persistence of vision'. Every image seen by the eyes remains visible for a fraction of a second after the image has gone. A film contains a series of still photographs taken a fraction of a second apart. When they are projected on to a screen, they appear so rapidly that persistence of vision transforms them into one moving picture.

Until the 1980s, motion pictures were produced entirely photographically. In 1982, the Disney film *Tron* added computer-generated backgrounds to film of actors. At first, digital movie clips were so expensive and time-consuming to produce that only small parts of images and short scenes could be created. But as the speed of computers increased and the cost of using them fell, longer and more complicated digital scenes could be produced.

Film

Lens

Shutter

The latest movie films have two soundtracks, one analogue and one digital. They are changed into electric current by shining a light through the film with a light-sensitive detector on the other side.

Inside a movie projector, each frame of film is pulled in front of the shutter, which moves round to let light shine through the film.

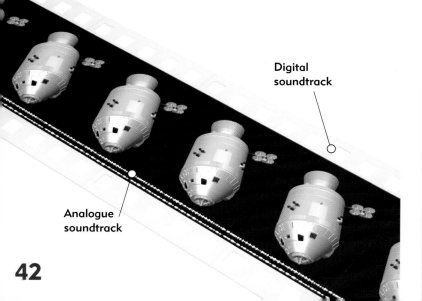

Digital soundtrack

Analogue soundtrack

TEST FILE

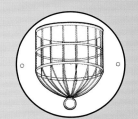

MAKE A THAUMATROPE

You can see how persistence of vision merges pictures together by making a thaumatrope. Cut out a circle of cardboard. Draw a picture on each side of the card. A bird on one side and a cage on the other work well. One picture must be upside down compared to the other. Tie a length of string to each side and spin the card. The two pictures should merge together.

Spinning this thaumatrope makes the two images appear to be one. The bird seems to be inside the cage.

Faster computers with big enough memories to handle photographic quality images became available to film-makers in the 1990s. They made it possible to create the amazingly realistic dinosaurs that appeared in *Jurassic Park* in 1993. Then in 1996, the first feature film to be created entirely by computer, *Toy Story*, was made.

From Sticks to Characters

To make a digital movie, the animators begin by making a storyboard – a series of drawings that show what happens in each scene. They start creating a scene using simple stick figures, because they are quick to work with. Once the characters' movements have been worked out, their 3D shape is built up on the stick figures. Then a 'mesh' that looks like wire netting is wrapped around the shape. Surface details, such as skin and clothes, and colour are added. Finally shadows and reflections are added. The film *Toy Story* took 800,000 hours of work on 300 computers to produce. Each minute of animation on the screen took about two days to create.

Digital effects are now commonplace in movies. They make starships fly through space and create armies of robots. The *Titanic* sailed again thanks to digital effects. And when the actor Oliver Reed died while *Gladiator* was being filmed, his scenes were finished by digitally combining existing film of his head with the body of another actor.

FACT FILE

COMPUTER ANIMATION
There are three types of computer animation – key-framing, motion capture and simulation. Movies like *Toy Story* are made by key-framing. Animators create the most important pictures (key frames) and computers create the 'in-between' pictures that link them together. Motion capture uses the movements of real people to animate digital characters. Simulation uses mathematical rules to work out how digital characters should move.

Aerial The part of a radio that transmits or receives radio waves.

Amplitude This is the size of the wave, such as a radio wave.

Antenna Another name for an aerial.

Binary code A code containing only two numbers – 0 and 1. All information is stored and processed by a computer in the form of binary code.

Carrier wave A radio wave used to carry information, such as someone's voice or a television picture.

Downlink The radio signal sent out by a satellite and received on Earth.

Electric current Electricity flowing through a wire or a piece of equipment.

Electromagnetic Having electric and magnetic parts. Electromagnetic waves, such as light and radio waves, are made of an electric wave and a magnetic wave travelling together.

Frequency The number of times a wave vibrates every second. One vibration per second is called one hertz, one thousand hertz is called one kilohertz and one million hertz is called one megahertz.

Ionosphere Part of the Earth's atmosphere, from 50 km to 1,000 km above the ground, that contains electrically charged particles.

Light year The distance light travels in one year, over 9 million million km. The vast distances to the stars are measured in light years.

Modem A modulator-demodulator; an electronic device for connecting a computer to a telephone line.

Modulate Change. A radio wave is modulated by adding another wave to it, to change its amplitude (size) or frequency (speed of vibration).

Network A group of things, such as computers, connected together.

Radar A system used to locate planes or ships that are too far away to see, by bouncing radio waves off them and detecting the reflections.

Receiver An electronic device for picking up radio waves.

Satellite An object in orbit around a planet. The moon is a natural satellite of the Earth. Orbiting spacecraft are artificial satellites.

Telecommunication Telegraph or telephone communication over long distances by means of electricity, light or radio waves.

Telemetry Obtaining measurements from a distance by radio or telephone.

Transmitter An electronic device for sending out radio waves from an aerial.

Uplink The radio signal sent up from the Earth to a satellite.

Wavelength The distance between the crest of one wave and the crest of the next wave.

World Wide Web Millions of documents available on the Internet connected together by 'clickable' links.

ORGANIZATIONS TO CONTACT

Museum of the Moving Image (MOMI)
South Bank Arts Centre, Waterloo, London SE1 8XT.
The development of film and television to the present day. Actor guides, and workshops for schools.

Science Museum
Exhibition Road, South Kensington, London SW7 2DD
Includes permanent collections on communications and computing; subjects include radio communications, telegraphs, telephones, computers and IT. There is also a collection on astronomy and space.

BOOKS TO READ

Century of Change: Communications by Jane Shuter (Heinemann, 1999)

Communications Close-Up: Film and Photography, Global Networks and Television and Radio by Ian Graham (Evans Brothers, 2000)

Communications: Invisible Journeys by Caroline Grimshaw (Two-Can, 1998)

Future Technology: Communications Now and into the Future by Steve Parker (Belitha, 1998)

Science Museum Book of Amazing Facts: Communications by Sarah Angliss (Hodder Children's Books, 1998)

WEB SITES

www.bt.com
Home page of British Telecom.

www.bbc.co.uk
Home page of the BBC, the world's first television broadcasting organization.

www.intelsat.com
Home page of Intelsat, an international communications satellite organization.

www.inmarsat.org
Home page of Inmarsat, the international maritime satellite organization, which mainly provides satellite services to shipping, but is also to available to others.

www.inventorsmuseum.com/comm.htm
An online inventors' museum showing the invention of the telegraph, telephone, television (including Farnsworth) and the invention of the computer.

www.kwarc.on.ca/hammond/marconi.html
An online museum dedicated to Marconi inventions.

www.nmsi.ac.uk/on-line/clarke
An online museum exhibit devoted to Arthur C. Clarke, inventor of the communications satellite.

INDEX

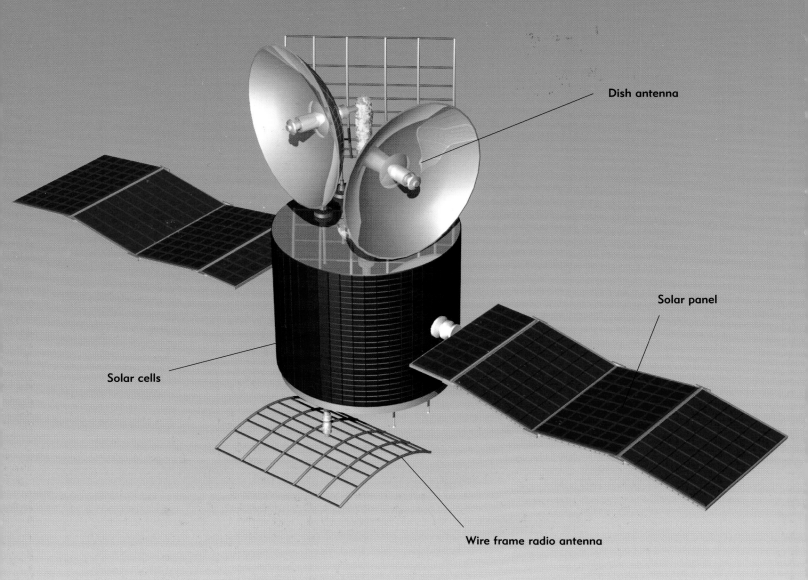

Dish antenna

Solar panel

Solar cells

Wire frame radio antenna

Communications satellite

**A communications satellite is fitted with
different sizes and shapes of radio
antennae to handle the different radio
signals it has to receive and re-transmit
back to Earth. The electricity needed to
power the radio equipment is made from
sunlight by thousands of solar cells.**